Merry, Merry Christmas to
Dear Barbie +
Caitlin + Cullen !

May you all — always —
enjoy the magic of looking
for Papa Noël !

Sincerely
Cécilia C. Dautry
+

Jenny

Cecilia Casrill Dartez

JENNY GIRAFFE
DISCOVERS
PAPA NOEL

Illustrated by Andy Green

PELICAN PUBLISHING COMPANY

Gretna 1994

To my maternal grandparents,
Camelia Navarro Gedoria and Inocincio Gedoria,
whose unconditional love and understanding
encouraged the unique growth of Jenny Giraffe and me

The word "Pelican" and the depiction of a pelican are trademarks
of Pelican Publishing Company, Inc.,
and are registered in the U.S. Patent and Trademark Office.

Library of Congress Cataloging-in-Publication Data

Dartez, Cecilia Casrill.
    Jenny Giraffe discovers Papa Noël / Cecilia Casrill Dartez ;
illustrated by Andy Green.
        p. cm.
    Summary: Jenny Giraffe's parents, teacher, and friends help her
learn about Papa Noël, during her first Christmas in New Orleans.
    ISBN 1-56554-084-0
    [1. Christmas—Fiction. 2. New Orleans (La.)—Fiction.
3. Animals—Fiction.] I. Green, Andy, ill. II. Title.
PZ7.D258Jd 1994
[E]—dc20   94-12719
                                                            CIP
                                                            AC

Manufactured in Korea
Published by Pelican Publishing Company, Inc.
1101 Monroe Street, Gretna, Louisiana 70053

JENNY GIRAFFE DISCOVERS PAPA NOEL

Jenny was going to meet her friends in Jackson Square when she finished her breakfast. Her adopted parents reminded her that it was wintertime.

"Wear this scarf, Jenny," said Claude. "This is winter, and it's cold outside."

"And . . . ," Angelle smiled, "wintertime means Christmas is coming. So, Papa Noël will be visiting us and bringing special presents."

Jenny shivered when she walked outside. "It is cold. And . . . this is my first winter in my new home." Then she thought, "So Christmas is coming, and Papa Noël will be bringing special presents. I have heard of these things, but . . . ," Jenny wondered, "I don't understand. Why do they really come?

As she continued to walk, Jenny became quite curious. "What is Christmas? Who is Papa Noël?"

She looked around and was extremely puzzled. "How do Christmas and Papa Noël come here? In a carriage? On a bus? In a taxi?"

When Jenny reached Jackson Square, she was very confused.

The park was filled with happy children, all busy drawing their wintertime pictures. Lita and T-Boy both wanted Jenny to see their drawings.

However, Jenny noticed the large decorated tree. "What is that strange tree?" she asked.

"Oh, Jenny," Lita laughed, "it's a Christmas tree. Christmas is almost here."

Jenny was now quite impatient with all the news about Christmas. "What is all this talk about Christmas?" she shouted. "What is Christmas? And who is Papa Noël?"

The teacher came over to help. "What is the matter, Jenny?"

"Oh, Miss Antoinette," wailed Jenny, "I don't understand Christmas."

Miss Antoinette smiled. "Christmas is a holiday season to celebrate the birth of a special baby—the Christ child. Baby Jesus Christ was born hundreds of years ago."

T-Boy comforted his friend. "Christmas is a wonderful time, Jenny. We have so many ways to celebrate the Baby Jesus' birthday."

"It's a very special birthday," said Miss Antoinette, "that people celebrate by going to their churches. The birth of the Baby Jesus was the promise of a new beginning for all people."

Jenny was still puzzled. "Does that mean we'll have a birthday party?"

Miss Antoinette smiled. "There are many Christmas parties, Jenny. But here in South Louisiana we also have other celebrations because of our French heritage." Then she added, "Let's all take Jenny to the Christmas parade next weekend."

Jenny could hardly wait.

On the morning of the Christmas parade, Jenny wore a new, bright-red beret with matching scarf. "Will I see Christmas and Papa Noël today?" she asked Claude and Angelle as they walked to the parade.

"The parade is only part of the Christmas celebration," Angelle answered. "Christmas Eve is when Papa Noël visits."

"Today," added Claude, "we'll see a special person dressed as Santa Claus to help welcome Christmas."

"Santa Claus?" asked Jenny as T-Boy ran over to join his friends.

"Santa Claus and Papa Noël are the same person," chirped T-Boy.

Angelle then explained that most American children know the Christmas visitor as "Santa Claus." However, Papa Noël's name came from the Louisiana French children of long ago.

Jenny was still puzzled.

"You see, Jenny, just like me," T-Boy suddenly thought. "My name is Tony, yet everyone calls me 'T-Boy.' But . . . I'm still the same person!"

Now Jenny understood, and was anxious to see the celebrity Santa Claus.

Soon, they reached the parade. Jenny could hardly believe the magnificent sight. There, high on a float, and in an enormous chair, sat the Santa Claus celebrity. He certainly was a jolly Santa.

The costumed float riders threw candy, gum, small toys, and beads for the eager crowd to catch.

School bands played loud, happy Christmas music.

Jenny decided that she was really going to enjoy her first Christmas.

The happy group walked home carrying bags filled with goodies they caught at the parade.

"Now . . . ," asked Jenny, "does Papa Noël visit us?"

"Not yet," answered Lita. "We still must do our Christmas caroling."

"Christmas caroling?" Again Jenny was curious.

Claude then explained about the Christmas caroling in Jackson Square. "Next Sunday, after we all go to our favorite churches, we'll meet at the park. There, we'll sing songs about the Baby Jesus, and songs about the Christmas holiday."

Jenny liked this idea because she loved to sing.

On Sunday evening, many people gathered at the park along with Jenny, her family, and friends. Everyone was given a candle and a song sheet.

When the church bells rang, the candles were lit, and the song leader announced the first song.

The joyful voices of hundreds of people could be heard throughout the French Quarter.

Even though Jenny still did not quite understand Christmas, she had a warm feeling inside that was very comforting.

As they walked home, again Jenny asked, "Now does Papa Noël visit us?"

"Oh, no," answered Lita. "On Christmas Eve, after we see the bonfires."

"Fires!" exclaimed Jenny.

Then Lita explained how grown-ups build large shapes out of firewood on the Mississippi River's levee. "And when the wood is lit," she continued, "the big fires light up the Christmas Eve sky so Papa Noël can find his way to bring our presents. In a few days we'll take a bus ride to the bonfires. Good night, Jenny."

Again, Jenny could hardly wait.

Christmas Eve finally arrived! Jenny, Claude, Angelle, and their friends took the long bus ride to the bonfires.

Jenny was still puzzled about the bonfires. "Why are fires used to light Papa Noël's way?"

"Winter in South Louisiana can sometimes be very foggy," Claude began. "So, many years ago, in the 1800s, the bonfire custom was started. People were concerned that Papa Noël could not find their homes. They then decided to build big fires next to the river to light his way."

Soon, the bus stopped. Everyone got off and walked up to the top of the levee to overlook the wide river.

"There goes the paddle-wheel boat!" shouted T-Boy. "Everyone on it is going to ride along the river to see more bonfires."

He proudly turned to Jenny. "Did you know that the Mississippi River is the longest river in the United States?"

"You mean the river goes to more states than just Louisiana?" asked Jenny.

"Dear Jenny," laughed Miss Antoinette, "the river goes through many states in our big and wonderful country."

Jenny stared thoughtfully at the riverboat. She quietly watched as it slowly moved along the river and out of sight. She decided that a riverboat would be her next watercolor painting.

"Come on!" shouted Lita. "The fires have been lit. Let's look for Papa Noël!"

The bright light from the bonfires lit the night sky like giant streetlights.

Everyone looked up. Everyone was quiet. Everyone watched and watched. Where was Papa Noël?

The light from the bonfires was shining brightly on the Mississippi River. The sparkling light on the water looked like hundreds of twinkling fairies dancing at a ball.

Still . . . no sign of Papa Noël.

Slowly, the bonfires became smaller and smaller until they were almost gone.

No one saw Papa Noël.

Soon, the night sky was dark again. The river was dark again.

Claude's voice startled Jenny. "Time to go. It's getting late."

"But," protested Jenny, "do you think Papa Noël saw the bonfires? Did he see us? Will he come here?"

"We'll know in the morning," yawned Angelle. "It is time to go home. We have quite a big day tomorrow—Christmas Day."

The bus ride home seemed so very long.

Many tired people got off the bus and walked quietly home. As they walked, Jenny remembered that this was the Baby Jesus' birthday.

The French Quarter neighborhood had a magical Christmas Eve look. Christmas lights were sparkling on doorways and balconies. "The lights are a beautiful birthday present," Jenny thought.

"Merry Christmas," friends called to each other as they parted.

Their own home seemed to have such a different and special feeling tonight. "Good night, Jenny," said Claude and Angelle. "May you have wonderful Christmas dreams."

"How can I sleep?" thought Jenny to herself. "Will Papa Noël really visit us? Does he know where I live?"

Hearing a noise, Jenny softly walked into the courtyard. The courtyard was lit with tiny Christmas lights in the tall banana plants. Filled with curiosity and expectation, Jenny looked all around.

There, on one of the banana plants, hung a stocking stuffed with some of her favorite fruit. A card was also in the stocking.

FOR JENNY

She read the card:

Merry Christmas, my dear Jenny. You must come visit me and meet my new friends. I wish you a beautiful Christmas.
I love you, my daughter.

Your Mama

P.S. Papa Noël is our very special friend.

"A card from my mother!" exclaimed Jenny. "I thought she was in the zoo. How did all this get here?"

Suddenly, Jenny heard a jingling sound overhead. She looked up into the night sky.
In the Christmas Eve moonlight . . . she saw him!
Papa Noël!
With his deep voice he called,

"Merry Christmas, Jenny!
Joyeux Noël to all!"